The Union Steward's Pocket Guide to Negotiating

Be Prepared at the Bargaining Table

Randy A. Speeg

Eldurhara Books

The Union Steward's Pocket Guide to Negotiating

Contents

1

Introduction to Union Contract Negotiations

*C*ollective *Bargaining Agreements* (aka *Union Contracts*) are a crucial aspect of labor relations. They determine the wages, benefits, and working conditions of the employees who are represented by a union. The process of negotiating a union contract can be complex and requires a thorough understanding of the collective bargaining process and the laws that govern it.

The purpose of this book is to provide an overview of union contract negotiations. We will explore the history of collective bargaining, the role of unions in the negotiation process, and the key elements of a union contract. We will also discuss the legal framework that governs union contract negotiations, including the rights and responsibilities of both management and labor.

The history of collective bargaining can be traced back to the 19th century, when workers began organizing to improve their wages and working conditions. Union membership and collective bargaining coverage increased during the 20th century, peaking in the 1950s. Since then, union membership has declined, but collective bargaining remains an important aspect of labor relations.

Unions are the employees' representative at the negotiation table. They are responsible for bargaining on behalf of the employees they represent. They are also responsible for enforcing the contract once it is signed. On the other hand, management is the representative of the employer and is responsible for negotiating on behalf of the employer.

A union contract, also known as a collective bargaining agreement, is a legally binding document that outlines the terms and conditions of employment for unionized employees. The contract typically includes provisions on wages, benefits, working conditions, and grievance and arbitration procedures.

The legal framework for union contract negotiations is established by the *National Labor Relations Act* (NLRA) in the United States. The NLRA guarantees the right of employees to form, join, or assist labor organizations and to engage in collective bargaining. The Act also establishes the rights and responsibilities of both management and labor in the negotiation process.

2

Before You Begin Negotiations

B efore you begin negotiations for a collective bargaining agreement there are several key steps that should first be taken.

Notify the Company of your intention to negotiate a new contract. This should typically be done no later than 60 days prior to the expiration of the existing contract. Most contracts will specify the time frame required for this notice to be made. If your existing contract specifies a time different than 60 days, then that is the timeframe that should be used. This step is essential to avoid legal complications from the employer attempting to halt negotiations due to a missed notification deadline.

Meet with Management to schedule the days and times for when negotiations will take place. You should also negotiate for a neutral site for the negotiations to take place and how the costs for the location will be split between the union and the company. Meeting on neutral grounds ensures that neither party has a logistical advantage over the other. Make sure that negotiations are scheduled far enough in advance that your team has the necessary time to prepare. It's also recommended that you schedule a separate *Housekeeping Meeting* to occur prior to the official negotiations. A housekeeping meeting is a meeting in which both parties will discuss and agree to ground rules for the negotiations, typically involving which individuals will be involved for both sides and an agreement that discussions at the negotiating table will remain confidential during the negotiating process, and any other details that might be pertinent to your specific situation. The Union should also use the housekeeping meeting to discuss and agree upon minor changes to the contract, such as cleaning up spelling errors and typos that may exist in the expiring contract. Agreeing upon these minor adjustments now will free up valuable time during the official negotiations. These agreements will of course be tentative and non-binding until the entire negotiation process has concluded.

File your F7 Notice of Collective Bargaining with the *Federal Mediation and Conciliation Service* at their website FMCS.gov. This step is required by law and necessary to ensure that you have certain legal protections in the negotiation process. The FMCS will also automatically assign a Mediator who will be available for use during the negotiations in case the parties come to an impasse and mutually agree to consult with the mediator. The mediator will not be present at the negotiations unless specifically asked by the parties but will remain on call during the entire process.

Form your Negotiation Committee. The negotiation committee will be the individuals who will be sitting at the negotiating table. Your negotiating committee should consist of the highest-ranking members of your union officers and stewards but may also consist of trusted members who are not serving as stewards. Great care should be taken in choosing the best individuals to represent the bargaining unit.

Analyze the Current Contract and identify the provisions that need to be changed, improved, or clarified. This may include wages, benefits, hours, seniority, health & safety, grievance procedures, etc. The negotiation committee should also review the past practices and grievances that have occurred under the current contract and how they can be prevented or resolved in the future.

Gather Input from the Members and find out what their priorities and concerns are. The negotiation committee should conduct surveys, meetings, interviews, or other methods to collect feedback from the workers and understand their needs and expectations. The negotiation committee should also educate the members about the bargaining process and their rights and responsibilities.

Research the Employer's Financial Situation and compare it with the industry standards and the market conditions. The negotiation committee should obtain relevant data and information that can support the union's proposals and counter the employer's arguments. This may include the employer's profits, revenues, expenses, productivity, market share, etc.

Develop Proposals and Arguments based on the contract analysis, the member input, and the financial research. The negotiation committee should draft clear and specific proposals that reflect the union's goals and demands. The committee should also prepare strong and persuasive arguments that justify the proposals and explain how they benefit both the workers and the employer.

Anticipate the Employer's Proposals and Arguments and prepare responses and counterproposals. The negotiation committee should try to predict what the employer will offer and ask for, and how they will try to persuade or pressure the union. The committee should also devise strategies and tactics to respond to the employer's moves and negotiate effectively.

Prepare for a Possible Strike or Lockout in case the negotiations reach an impasse, or the employer engages in unfair labor practices. The union should inform the members about the legal and practical aspects of a strike or lockout, and organize them to participate in potential picketing, rallies, or other actions. The union should also coordinate with other unions, community groups, or media outlets to gain support and solidarity.

3

Understanding the Collective Bargaining Process

C ollective bargaining is the process by which unions and management negotiate the terms and conditions of employment for unionized employees. It is a fundamental aspect of labor relations and plays a crucial role in determining the wages, benefits, and working conditions of unionized employees. Collective bargaining is the process by which unions and management negotiate the terms and conditions of employment for unionized employees. It is a fundamental aspect of labor relations and plays a crucial role in determining the wages, benefits, and working conditions of unionized employees.

The collective bargaining process is complex and time-consuming, but it is essential for both management and labor to understand the process in order to negotiate effectively. This chapter will provide an overview of the collective bargaining process and explore the key stages of negotiation.

The first stage of the collective bargaining process is preparing for negotiations. This involves researching the current economic and industry trends, as well as the specific needs and concerns of the union and management. Both sides also develop their negotiation strategies and identify their priorities.

The second stage is the negotiation itself. This is where the union and management come together to discuss and negotiate the terms of the contract. The negotiation process will be difficult and may involve compromise and concessions on both sides of the table.

The third stage is the drafting of the contract. Once an agreement has been reached, the contract is written and reviewed by both sides. The contract includes the terms and conditions of employment, such as wages, benefits, and working conditions, as well as any other agreements that were reached during negotiations.

The fourth stage is the ratification process. Once the contract is written, it is presented to the union membership for a vote. If the contract is ratified, it becomes legally binding and is enforced by both the union and management.

It's worth mentioning that the collective bargaining process can be different from one industry to another, and there could be variations depending on the country and the laws that govern the labor relations.

The fifth stage is the contract administration. Once the contract is ratified, it becomes legally binding, and both the union and management are responsible for enforcing its terms and conditions. This stage involves monitoring compliance with the contract, addressing any issues that arise via the grievance process, and making any necessary adjustments to the contract or remedies to the affected parties.

The sixth stage is the contract renewal process. At the end of the contract term, the union and management must come together again to negotiate a new contract. This stage involves reviewing the terms and conditions of the current contract, identifying any changes that are needed or wanted, and starting the negotiation process again.

It's important to note that the collective bargaining process can be challenging and it's not uncommon for negotiations to reach an impasse. An impasse occurs when the union and management are unable to reach an agreement on important issues. When this happens, both sides have several options, such as mediation or binding arbitration, to help resolve the impasse.

It's also important to note that collective bargaining is not always smooth, and it's not uncommon for negotiations to be disrupted by strikes, lockouts, or other forms of labor unrest. A strike is when the employees refuse to work until their demands are met, while a lockout is when the employer prohibits the employees from working until their demands are met.

Understanding the collective bargaining process is essential for both management and labor to negotiate effectively and arrive at a fair and mutually beneficial contract agreement.

4

Preparing for Negotiations: Research and Strategy

T he key to a successful union contract negotiation is preparation. Both management and labor need to conduct research and develop a negotiation strategy before they begin the actual negotiation process. This chapter will explore the importance of research and strategy in the negotiation process and provide tips on how to prepare effectively.

The first step in preparing for negotiations is to conduct research. Both management and labor need to gather information about the current economic and industry trends, as well as the specific needs and concerns of the union and management. This includes researching the wages, benefits, and working conditions of similar companies in the industry, as well as the history of the current contract and any past negotiations.

Once the research is done, both sides should develop a negotiation strategy. This includes identifying the key issues that need to be addressed, setting priorities, and determining the best approach for achieving the desired outcome. Management and labor should also consider the strengths and weaknesses of their own positions, and anticipate the positions of the other side.

It's important for management and labor to have a clear understanding of their objectives and expectations, and be prepared to present their position in a clear and convincing way. Both sides should also be prepared to compromise and make concessions in order to reach an agreement.

It's also a good idea to prepare a team of representatives that will negotiate on behalf of the management or the labor. This team should be composed of individuals with the necessary knowledge and skills to negotiate effectively, and should be led by a chief negotiator who will be responsible for coordinating the team's efforts.

In addition, both management and labor should consider what their best and worst case scenarios are, and plan accordingly. This includes identifying any possible obstacles to the negotiation and developing strategies to overcome them.

Furthermore, it's important for both sides to have a clear understanding of the legal framework that governs union contract negotiations, including the rights and responsibilities of both management and labor under the law. This knowledge can help both sides to identify any potential legal issues that may arise during negotiations, and to develop strategies to address them.

It's also beneficial to have a good understanding of the current labor market, including the availability of skilled workers, the level of unemployment, and the economic conditions in the region. This information can be used to assess the strength of the union and management's positions, and to anticipate the likely demands and concessions of the other side.

Another important aspect of preparation is to be aware of the history of the current contract and any past negotiations. This includes understanding the previous agreements, the reasons for past disputes and the way they were resolved. This knowledge can help to identify any potential sticking points, and to develop strategies to address them.

In addition, both management and labor should be prepared to use various negotiation tactics and techniques, such as the use of objective criteria, the use of interest-based negotiation, the use of objective criteria, and the use of mediation or binding arbitration to resolve impasse.

Another important aspect of preparation is to establish clear communication channels with the union and management. This includes setting up regular meetings, creating a shared agenda for the negotiation process, and agreeing on the format for the negotiations. Clear communication can help to reduce the potential for misunderstandings and can help to build trust between both sides.

It's also important to keep in mind that negotiations can take time and both sides need to be prepared for the process to take several weeks, months, or even longer. Both management and labor should be prepared to be patient and to maintain a positive attitude throughout the process.

Finally, it's important for both management and labor to be aware of the power dynamics in the negotiation process. This includes understanding the relative bargaining power of both sides and the impact that this can have on the negotiation. Both sides should be aware of the potential for power imbalances and should work to address them.

Preparing for union contract negotiations is crucial for achieving a fair and mutually beneficial agreement. Both sides should conduct research, develop a negotiation strategy, have a clear understanding of the legal framework, be aware of the current labor market, the history of the current contract and any past negotiations, establish clear communication channels, be prepared for the process to take time and be aware of the power dynamics in the negotiation process. By preparing effectively, both management and labor can negotiate more confidently and effectively, resulting in a successful negotiation.

5

Effective Communication Techniques for the Negotiation Table

E ffective communication is a crucial aspect of union contract negotiations. It allows both management and labor to effectively express their positions, understand the positions of the other side, and reach a mutually beneficial agreement. This chapter will explore effective communication techniques that can be used at the negotiation table. It's also important to use clear and concise language when communicating at the negotiation table. This includes avoiding jargon or technical language that the other side may not understand. Clear and concise language can help to reduce the potential for misunderstandings and can make it easier for the other side to understand your position.

Active Listening

The first technique is active listening. This involves fully listening to the other side and understanding their position and concerns, and showing that you are fully engaged in the conversation., rather than just focusing on expressing your own position. Active listening allows both sides to understand the concerns and priorities of the other side, which can help to build trust and increase the likelihood of reaching an agreement.

Active listening involves paying attention not only to the words spoken but also to the nonverbal cues and the underlying emotions and intentions. This includes observing the speaker's body language, tone of voice, and the context of the conversation. By paying attention to these cues, it's possible to gain a deeper understanding of the other side's position, concerns, and priorities.

To actively listen, it's important to avoid interrupting the speaker, refrain from formulating a response while the other person is talking and avoid getting defensive. Instead, it's better to listen attentively, ask clarifying questions, and paraphrase what the other person has said to confirm your understanding.

Active listening can help to build trust and rapport between the two sides. It demonstrates that you are genuinely interested in understanding the other side's perspective and that you value their input. This can lead to a more productive and collaborative negotiation process and increase the likelihood of reaching a mutually beneficial agreement.

Additionally, active listening can help to identify potential areas of agreement and to mitigate potential conflicts. By understanding the other side's concerns and priorities, it's possible to find common ground and develop creative solutions that meet the needs of both sides.

Objective Criteria

The use of objective criteria is an effective communication technique that can be used at the negotiation table to support a position and to reduce the potential for misunderstandings. Objective criteria refers to the use of data and facts to support a position, rather than relying on emotions or subjective opinions. This can help to make a position more convincing and can provide a basis for rational discussion.

When using objective criteria, it's important to ensure that the data and facts used are accurate and reliable. This includes checking the source of the information, verifying its accuracy and relevance, and providing context and explanation when necessary.

One way to use objective criteria is to present data and statistics that demonstrate the impact of a particular issue on the company or the union. For example, if management is proposing a change to the health insurance benefits, they can present data on the costs of the current plan and the projected savings of the proposed plan. This can help to make the case for the proposed change and to provide a basis for discussion.

Another way to use objective criteria is to present industry standards or best practices. For example, if the union is proposing changes to the safety protocols in the workplace, they can present data on the industry standard for safety protocols and how the company's current protocols compare. This can help to make the case for the proposed changes and to provide a basis for discussion.

The use of objective criteria can also be helpful in resolving impasse. By providing data and facts, both sides can better understand each other's positions and can work towards finding a solution that addresses the underlying concerns and priorities.

Interest-based Negotiation

Interest-based negotiation is a technique that can be used at the negotiation table to effectively communicate and reach a mutually beneficial agreement. This approach focuses on the underlying interests of both sides, rather than just focusing on their positions. By understanding the interests of the other side, both management and labor can develop creative solutions that meet the needs of both sides.

Interest-based negotiation is also called "win-win" negotiation, as it aims to find a solution that satisfies both parties' needs and concerns. This approach is different from traditional "win-lose" negotiation, where one party's gain is another party's loss.

In interest-based negotiation, the focus is on understanding the underlying interests, needs, and concerns of the parties involved. This includes identifying the reasons why a particular position is important to the other side, and finding ways to address those interests.

To use this technique, both management and labor should be willing to explore the other side's interests, be open to new ideas and be flexible in their approach. It's important to be prepared to listen actively, to ask open-ended questions, and to be willing to consider options that were not initially considered.

Interest-based negotiation can also be used to resolve impasse. By focusing on the underlying interests, both sides can identify potential areas of agreement and develop creative solutions that meet the needs of both sides.

Open-ended Questions

The use of open-ended questions is another effective communication technique that can be used at the negotiation table to encourage dialogue and understanding. Open-ended questions are questions that cannot be answered with a simple "yes" or "no" response, and require the person being asked to provide a more detailed answer.

Open-ended questions can be used to encourage the other side to share their thoughts, feelings and concerns. This can help to understand the other side's perspective and to identify potential areas of agreement.

For example, management can use open-ended questions to understand the union's concerns about working conditions, such as "Can you tell me more about the specific issues that the union members are facing in the workplace?" or "What are the main factors that are affecting the union members' morale and productivity?"

Similarly, the union can use open-ended questions to understand management's concerns about costs, such as "Can you explain in more detail the financial challenges that the company is facing?" or "What are the main factors that are affecting the company's ability to compete in the market?"

Using open-ended questions can also help to reduce the potential for misunderstandings and to build trust and rapport between the two sides. This can lead to a more productive and collaborative negotiation process and increase the likelihood of reaching a mutually beneficial agreement.

Effective communication is a crucial aspect of union contract negotiations. It allows both management and labor to effectively express their positions, understand the positions of the other side, and reach a mutually beneficial agreement. Techniques such as active listening, the use of objective criteria, interest-based negotiation, clear and concise language, and open-ended questions, can help both sides communicate effectively at the negotiation table. By using these techniques, both management and labor can negotiate more confidently and effectively, resulting in a successful negotiation.

6

Managing Conflict and Building Consensus

C onflict is a natural part of the negotiation process and can arise from a variety of sources, such as differences in interests, values, and perceptions. Managing conflict and building consensus is an important aspect of union contract negotiations and is crucial for achieving a fair and mutually beneficial agreement. This chapter will explore strategies for managing conflict and building consensus during union contract negotiations.

One of the most effective strategies for managing conflict is to address it directly and early on. This includes identifying the source of the conflict, understanding the interests and concerns of both sides, and developing a plan to address the issues.

Another strategy is to use interest-based negotiation. This approach focuses on the underlying interests of both sides, rather than just focusing on their positions. By understanding the interests of the other side, both management and labor can develop creative solutions that meet the needs of both sides and reduce the potential for conflict.

It's also important to use effective communication techniques, such as active listening and the use of objective criteria, to reduce the potential for misunderstandings and to build trust and rapport between the two sides.

Another strategy for managing conflict is to build consensus. Consensus building is the process of creating agreement among all parties involved, in which all parties feel that their concerns have been addressed and that the solution reached is fair and mutually beneficial.

One way to build consensus is to use a collaborative problem-solving approach, in which both management and labor work together to find a solution that addresses the concerns of both sides. This includes identifying the shared interests, brainstorming potential solutions, and evaluating the options based on objective criteria.

Another way to build consensus is to use a democratic decision-making process, in which both management and labor have an equal opportunity to participate in the decision-making process. This includes setting up a voting process, in which both sides can vote on the proposed solutions and using a majority vote to determine the final agreement.

It's also important to keep in mind that building consensus takes time and patience. Both management and labor should be prepared to engage in a dialogue and to be open to new ideas.

When an impasse is reached a good strategy is to use mediation or binding arbitration to resolve the impasse. Mediation is a process where a neutral third party helps the two sides to communicate effectively and to reach a mutually acceptable agreement, while binding arbitration is a process where a neutral third party makes a decision that is binding on both sides. Mediation is a voluntary process, and both sides need to agree to participate in it.

A mediator's role is to facilitate communication between the two sides, and to help them to identify the underlying interests and concerns. The mediator can also help to identify potential areas of agreement, and to develop creative solutions that meet the needs of both sides. Mediators do not impose solutions on the parties, they help them to find a mutually acceptable agreement.

One of the advantages of using a mediator is that they are able to provide an objective perspective on the issues at hand. They are not emotionally involved in the process and can help to identify areas of misunderstanding and potential solutions.

Another advantage of using a mediator is that they can help to create a more positive and productive negotiation climate, by fostering open communication and mutual respect between the two sides. This can help to reduce the potential for conflict and to increase the likelihood of reaching a mutually beneficial agreement.

Using a mediator can also be a cost-effective solution to resolving impasse, as it can save time and money compared to traditional forms of dispute resolution such as going to court or taking legal action.

In conclusion, managing conflict and building consensus is an important aspect of union contract negotiations. Strategies such as addressing conflict directly and early on, using interest-based negotiation, effective communication techniques, mediation or binding arbitration, and building consensus through collaborative problem-solving and democratic decision-making, can help to reduce the potential for conflict and to reach a fair and mutually beneficial agreement. By managing conflict and building consensus effectively, both management and labor can negotiate more confidently and effectively, resulting in a successful negotiation.

7

Wage and Benefit Negotiations

Wages and benefits are often among the most contentious issues in union contract negotiations. Both management and labor have strong interests in these areas, and it's important to approach these negotiations with a clear understanding of the issues at hand. This chapter will explore strategies for negotiating wages and benefits during union contract negotiations.

One of the most important strategies for negotiating wages and benefits is to conduct thorough research. This includes understanding the current labor market, researching comparable wages and benefits in the industry, and analyzing the company's financial situation. This information can be used to support your position and to provide a basis for rational discussion.

Another strategy is to use objective criteria to evaluate the proposed wages and benefits. This includes analyzing the impact of the proposed wages and benefits on the company's financial situation and on the union members' standard of living. By using objective criteria, both management and labor can make informed decisions and avoid basing decisions on emotions or subjective opinions.

It's also important to keep in mind that wages and benefits are not only about money, but also about the overall compensation package. This includes considering non-monetary benefits such as retirement plans, health insurance, vacation time, and other perks. Both management and labor should be open to exploring different options and to finding creative solutions that meet the needs of both sides.

Another strategy for negotiating wages and benefits is to use interest-based negotiation. This approach focuses on the underlying interests of both sides, rather than just focusing on their positions. By understanding the interests of the other side, both management and labor can develop creative solutions that meet the needs of both sides.

In conclusion, negotiating wages and benefits during union contract negotiations can be a complex and challenging task. It's important to conduct thorough research, use objective criteria, be open to exploring different options, use interest-based negotiation, and approach the negotiation with a clear understanding of the issues at hand.

Negotiating for retirement plans, health insurance, vacation time, and other perks is also an important aspect of union contract negotiations. These non-monetary benefits are often just as important as wages and can have a significant impact on the overall compensation package.

Retirement plans, such as defined benefit plans and defined contribution plans, are an important consideration in union contract negotiations. Both management and labor need to carefully consider the costs, benefits, and risks associated with these plans, and to find a solution that meets the needs of both sides.

Health insurance is another key benefit that is often negotiated in union contract negotiations. Both management and labor need to consider the costs, coverage options, and the impact of the proposed plan on the union members' standard of living.

Vacation time is also an important benefit that is often negotiated in union contract negotiations. Both management and labor need to consider the needs of the union members, and to find a solution that meets the needs of both sides.

Other perks such as flexible work arrangements, educational opportunities, and professional development programs are also important benefits that can be negotiated in union contract negotiations. These benefits can have a positive impact on employee satisfaction and productivity and can be an important part of the overall compensation package.

Negotiating for retirement plans, health insurance, vacation time, and other perks is an important aspect of union contract negotiations. Both management and labor need to consider the costs, benefits, and risks associated with these benefits, and to find a solution that meets the needs of both sides. By negotiating for these non-monetary benefits, both management and labor can negotiate more confidently and effectively, resulting in a fair and mutually beneficial agreement.

8

Grievance and Arbitration Procedures

Grievance and arbitration procedures are an essential aspect of union contract negotiations. These procedures provide a mechanism for addressing and resolving disputes that may arise between management and labor. This chapter will explore strategies for negotiating grievance and arbitration procedures during union contract negotiations.

One of the most important strategies for negotiating grievance and arbitration procedures is to establish clear and concise language that defines the process. This includes outlining the steps involved in filing a grievance, timelines for resolution, and the roles and responsibilities of both management and labor. Clear and concise language can help to reduce the potential for misunderstandings and to increase the likelihood of a timely and fair resolution.

Establish a clear and objective standard for determining the outcome of a grievance or arbitration. This can include using objective criteria such as company policies, industry standards, and relevant laws to evaluate the merits of a grievance or arbitration. By using clear and objective standards, both management and labor can make informed decisions and avoid basing decisions on emotions or subjective opinions.

It's also important to establish a clear and impartial process for selecting arbitrators. This can include using a neutral third party, such as the American Arbitration Association, to select arbitrators, or establishing a pool of qualified arbitrators from which to choose. Clear and impartial processes for selecting arbitrators can help to ensure that the arbitration is fair and unbiased.

Another strategy for negotiating grievance and arbitration procedures is to establish a system of progressive discipline. This can include a series of escalating steps, such as verbal warnings, written warnings, and suspension or termination, that are taken in response to repeated or serious violations of company policies or standards. Progressive discipline can help to ensure that disputes are resolved in a fair and consistent manner.

In conclusion, negotiating grievance and arbitration procedures during union contract negotiations is an essential aspect of the negotiation process. By establishing clear and concise language, clear and objective standards, clear and impartial process for selecting arbitrators, and a system of progressive discipline, both management and labor can ensure that disputes are resolved in a timely, fair and efficient manner. Additionally, by having a clear process in place, both management and labor can avoid potential conflicts and misunderstandings and focus on maintaining a positive and productive working relationship.

It's also important to note that both management and labor should be trained on the grievance and arbitration procedures to ensure that they are familiar with the process and their respective roles and responsibilities. This can help to ensure that the process runs smoothly and that disputes are resolved in a timely and effective manner.

In addition, it's important to establish a mechanism for appeals in case a party disagree with the outcome of the arbitration, this can be done by including the right of either party to appeal the decision to a higher level of authority, such as a higher management or a court of law.

Grievance and arbitration procedures are an essential aspect of union contract negotiations, they provide a mechanism for addressing and resolving disputes that may arise between management and labor. By establishing clear and concise language, clear and objective standards, clear and impartial process for selecting arbitrators, a system of progressive discipline, and a mechanism for appeals, both management and labor can ensure that disputes are resolved in a timely, fair, efficient and impartial manner.

9

The Role of Government and Labor Laws in Contract Negotiations

The role of government and labor laws in union contract negotiations is an important aspect to consider. These laws establish the rights and responsibilities of both management and labor, and they can have a significant impact on the negotiation process. This chapter will explore the role of government and labor laws in union contract negotiations.

One of the most important government laws that applies to union contract negotiations is the *National Labor Relations Act* (NLRA). This law guarantees the right of employees to form, join, or assist labor organizations, and to engage in collective bargaining. The NLRA also prohibits certain types of employer and union conduct, such as interfering with employees' rights to form, join, or assist labor organizations. Understanding the NLRA is crucial for both management and labor as it sets the basic framework for collective bargaining.

Another important law is the *Fair Labor Standards Act* (FLSA), which establishes minimum wage and overtime pay standards. The FLSA applies to both union and non-union workplaces, and it's important for management and labor to understand their rights and responsibilities under this law.

There are also state labor laws that can impact union contract negotiations. These laws can vary from state to state, and it's important for both management and labor to be familiar with the specific laws in their state.

It's also important to consider the impact of other laws such as the *Americans with Disabilities Act* (ADA), the *Family and Medical Leave Act* (FMLA), and the *Occupational Safety and Health Act* (OSHA) on union contract negotiations. These laws establish rights and responsibilities for both management and labor, and it's important for both sides to understand their impact on the negotiation process.

Government and labor laws play a significant role in union contract negotiations. It's important for both management and labor to be familiar with the laws that apply to their workplace, such as the NLRA, FLSA, state labor laws, and other laws such as the ADA, FMLA, and OSHA. By understanding the laws that apply to their workplace, both management and labor can negotiate more confidently and effectively and ensure that the contract is in compliance with the law.

It's also important to note that government agencies such as the *National Labor Relations Board* (NLRB) and the *Department of Labor* (DOL) are responsible for enforcing labor laws, and they play an important role in the negotiation process. Both management and labor should be familiar with the processes and procedures of these agencies and should seek legal counsel if they have any questions or concerns.

Additionally, both management and labor should be aware of the potential impact of any proposed changes in labor laws and regulations that may occur during the term of the contract, this could affect the negotiation process and the outcome of the contract. Therefore, it's important to keep up to date with any changes in labor laws and regulations.

In conclusion, the role of government and labor laws in union contract negotiations is an important aspect to consider. By understanding the laws that apply to their workplace, both management and labor can negotiate more confidently and effectively, ensure that the contract is in compliance with the law, and be aware of the potential impact of any proposed changes in labor laws and regulations. This can help to ensure a fair and mutually beneficial agreement for both management and labor.

10

Finalizing and Ratifying the Collective Bargaining Agreement

Finalizing and ratifying a collective bargaining agreement is the last step in the negotiation process. This chapter will explore strategies for finalizing and ratifying your brand-new union contract.

One of the most important strategies for finalizing a union contract is to ensure that both management and labor have reached a comprehensive and mutually beneficial agreement. This includes reviewing the contract language and ensuring that all key issues have been addressed and resolved, nothing has been overlooked, and that no errors have been made. It's also important to ensure that the contract is in compliance with all applicable laws and regulations.

Another strategy is to involve all relevant parties in the finalization process. This includes management and labor representatives, legal counsel, and any other stakeholders that have an interest in the agreement. Involving all relevant parties can help to ensure that the contract is fair, comprehensive, and legally compliant.

Once the contract is finalized, it's important to present the agreement to the union members for ratification. This includes providing the union members with a detailed explanation of the agreement and giving them an opportunity to ask questions and express any concerns. It's also important to provide the union members with a clear and concise summary of the contract and an explanation of the voting process.

Once the contract is ratified, both management and labor must take the necessary steps to implement the agreement. This includes communicating the agreement to all employees, making any necessary changes to company policies and procedures, and ensuring that all employees are aware of their rights and responsibilities under the contract.

Another important strategy for finalizing and ratifying a union contract is to establish a clear implementation plan and timeline. This should include specific deadlines for communication, training, and any necessary changes to company policies and procedures. This will ensure that the agreement is implemented in a timely and efficient manner and that both management and labor are held accountable for meeting the established deadlines.

It's also important to establish a mechanism for ongoing communication and collaboration between management and labor. This can include regular meetings, a joint committee, or other forms of communication to ensure that any issues or concerns are addressed in a timely manner. This can help to maintain a positive and productive working relationship between management and labor and to ensure that the contract is being implemented as intended.

Additionally, it's also important to establish a mechanism for contract enforcement. This can include a dispute resolution process, a grievance procedure, or a process for arbitration. This will ensure that both management and labor have a way to address any potential violations or non-compliance with the contract. Best practice is to negotiate and include this grievance procedure within the actual contract itself to ensure that following the procedure is legally binding.

Finalizing and ratifying the contract is the last critical step in the negotiation process. By having a clear implementation plan and timeline, establishing a mechanism for ongoing communication and collaboration, and a mechanism for contract enforcement, both management and labor can ensure that the contract is being implemented as intended and that any issues or concerns are addressed in a timely manner. This can help to maintain a positive and productive working relationship between management and labor and to ensure the contract is successfully enforced.

Afterword

Negotiating for collective bargaining agreements can be a complex and challenging process, but it's an essential aspect of maintaining a positive and productive working relationship between management and labor. This book has provided an overview of the key strategies and best practices for negotiating, including understanding the collective bargaining process, preparing for negotiations, effective communication techniques, managing conflict and building consensus, and the role of government and labor laws in contract negotiations.

As you've read, effective negotiation requires thorough research, the use of objective criteria, effective communication techniques, and a focus on the underlying interests of both management and labor. It's also important to be familiar with the laws and regulations that apply to union contract negotiations, and to be aware of the potential impact of any proposed changes in labor laws and regulations.

By following the strategies and best practices outlined in this book, both management and labor can negotiate more confidently and effectively and reach a fair and mutually beneficial agreement. With a well-negotiated contract, both management and labor can work together towards the common goal of a successful and productive workplace.

About the Author

Randy A. Speeg has been Unit Vice President of the International Chemical Workers Union Council of the United Food and Commercial Workers International Union (ICWUC/UFCW) Local 664C since 2006, serving the employees of the Totes Isotoner Corporation in Cincinnati, Ohio.

Also by

Randy A. Speeg

The Union Steward's Field Book: A Pocket Guide to Dealing with Management

www.ingramcontent.com/pod-product-compliance
Lightning Source LLC
Chambersburg PA
CBHW060005300526
45794CB00003B/1099